Chapter 1	Mental mindset	
Chapter 2	Be a concierge	
Chapter 3	Appreciation for your guests	
Chapter 4	Make them like you	
Chapter 5	Build trust	
Chapter 6	Know your product	
Chapter 7	As humans we follow trends	
Chapter 8	Asking is easy	
Chapter 9	Objections	
Chapter 10	3 easy rules to follow	

Chapter 1 – Mental mindset

Our attitude is everything in this business. How often do you see grumpy people succeed? It's always the go-getter. Always the happy and overly positive that make money in our business. Why? People are attracted to and listen to us when we are happy and positive. Be happy and excited for them in the moment and make them feel special.

Would you want the doctor you are seeing to have a negative attitude and to be in a bad mood? Of course not. I'm sure we all have had an interaction with someone who had a bad attitude. Our impression of the experience whether it was a doctor visit, restaurant, coffee shop, grocery store, anything that made us unhappy or uncomfortable ruins that image for future visits.

We need to make the experience for our guests a great one. They like us and they'll like what we are offering. Negative energy attracts negative energy. Positive energy attracts positive energy. Ever have a day where everything goes wrong? So what if you didn't book a tour yesterday, book two more tomorrow. Don't dwell on it. You know how to do your job. You can and will succeed.

You can and will succeed! Tell yourself this over and over and over. Wake up in the morning and smile. A positive attitude every day is important. Think of all the other jobs you have had or all the other jobs out there that you could be doing.

Be grateful for your new found career. Be grateful for the money that will come your way. Be grateful for the quality of vacations that you will be introducing people to. I know this sounds like drinking the proverbial "lemonade", but it is not. This is what you must do. What is the one thing we all want to do? The answer is to take vacations and get away from the daily grind of life. Even if it's an extra day off or a mini 3 day vacation. This is what you are providing for your guests. This is the mindset you must have day in and day out.

Remember with good thoughts, great things will come your way. Don't push it. Don't stress about it. Just have fun.

Whatever is going on in your life you must check all that at the door when you show up to work. Enjoy life and take vacations yourself. Just have fun. Live life to have fun. Be fun.

Chapter 2 – Be a concierge

First and foremost we need to assist our guests as best we can. Find out what they like to do rather than what someone told them to do. It's easy to suggest ideas for them. This is a great opportunity for discovery questions.

Ask questions to find out:
Where they have vacationed?
Where they prefer to vacation?
What brought them out to their current destination?
Why they chose to stay with us?
What do they want to do here?
Have they had any recommendations from anyone else?

If you are giving gifts for a presentation then align any one of those gifts to their plans. Perhaps they have everything booked already then offer them a way to save some money at the resort with resort credits or if they are part of a points program then offer them free points. You ask many questions to determine what my be a greater value to them. There is absolutely no reason to go through every single gift and waste their time.

It helps to have been in the hospitality industry for many years. Being a concierge sounds easy and it will be. Starting off isn't easy. If I had this knowledge when I started I would have excelled from the beginning. Now with years of experience, trial and error, lots of money and some awards here and there I bring this knowledge. What is important is what you will take away from this book. Whether you are starting off new or have been in the business for many years.

Take what I am going to teach you and adopt it directly or adopt it in your style but please stick to the basics. This industry is a show and you are the entertainer. The idea is to remain who you are and enjoy what you do…and when the guest is in front of you put on that smile and entertain.

Do we have an ulterior motive? Absolutely! We want to get them on tour and we want them to join our program.

After all timeshare and fractional ownership are life changing. Imagine your guests having the ability to vacation more often with better quality and being proud that they have secured a lifetime of luxury. All this while providing superior guest service. I will explain more about this further in the chapters.

I will also share with you a variety of practical applications to use the methods I am presenting. Unlike this book, most sales books lack the practical side and are not representative of the concierge field.

I hope you enjoy the success that will come your way.

Be efficient with their time. As much fun as you may be having with them always remember they are on vacation and even though they may be smiling they might just want to get back to having fun. So if they are planning one excursion and you happen to be gifting that for a presentation then align your invitation to tour with that gift. If they plan on dining on property or having drinks by the pool then use the resort credit. The only way we can determine what's best for them is by asking. If you don't engage with your guests and think that they are amazing then don't bother showing up for work and find a new job. Once you lose that appreciation for your guests the money goes away.

It's their time and time is money. It's also your time too. The sooner you can assist your guest and book them on tour the sooner you can help the next guest. Always be sure to leave ample time to talk about the presentation. Time closing yourself is the worst. If you are not familiar with a "time close" allow me to explain. You spend a couple minutes talking about their stay, another few minutes about what they want to do, many more talking about activities and all of sudden they want to leave. We are on their schedule, but there are a few things we can do to put them on your schedule which will be discussed further in the chapters.

There is nothing worse than trying to speed up your invitation for them to go on a presentation. It seems rushed because you are forcing it and the guests will pick up on that and it will seem awkward. Ways around that are simple. Two ways to avoid this all together are:

Example 1:
I've mentioned this before about aligning a gift. While you are speaking with them and one of your gifts is a perfect fit for an activity then by all means tell them. Make it authentic and that you have their best interests at heart.

"So I've got an idea and everyone I speak with loves this. I'm sure you're aware this is an ownership property and I always invite my guests on a really fun presentation to experience a new way to vacation. You mentioned that you wanted to go see this show. Well if you like to vacation and spend a really quick 90 minutes with us then we'd like to pay for that for you. That would free up some of your cash for another dinner or another activity. Let's circle back to that and talk about some other things that you are interested in. I do recommend booking the show while you're here with me since it's very popular and fills up quickly." Then continue assisting them.

Urgency is everything so whatever it may be, even a timeshare presentation, everything books up quick. When you circle back to the invitation be excited for them and tell them how much fun they'll have at the show.

Example 2:
If you are unable to get the invitation out till the very end then make it seem as if you would feel bad for not at least sharing it with them.

"One last thing I'd like to share with you. I get the impression that you like to vacation. Is that correct? Perfect. Then like most of my guests that do like to vacation they always like to do one of our presentations here because of the free gift you get. Our tours are quick, 90 minutes and no pressure plus because we are so proud of our staff we always do a followup survey to make sure you had a great time. They're fun and interactive and you can choose from one of these gifts. If you have just 90 minutes I say go in and check us out and get the free gift. Looking at your itinerary it looks like either tomorrow morning or afternoon works. I have a spot at 8:30 or 12:30. Which one works best for you? Oh and which gift would you like?"

The previous sentence is risky? It leaves an out for them. It leaves them with an option to say no. Assumptive close them instead of giving them that option to say no. A great example would be: "It sounds like you prefer to get up early. Lots of my guests love the early times so I think the 8:30am tour time would work pretty well. You mentioned that you want to enjoy the restaurants here so the resort credit would help save you some money and enjoy some extra meals. Would you like tomorrow or the next day?"

What happened here is that you removed "no thank you" from the entire closing process and kept their best interests at heart which makes you appear sincere and care for them. You still gave them a choice but instead of yes or no, it's assumptive that they are going to tour but on which day?

Choice is something as humans we must have. The instant choice is removed from us we feel trapped. We simply take that choice and mold it to work for us and from your guests point of view they were free to make a choice.

Again….always make it fun. Always. Always. Always. Keep up the energy.

Chapter 3 – Appreciation for your guests

We love our guests. Love them! After all they do pay our bills. They spend money to enjoy their vacation. They spend money to be with each other as a couple or as a family or for experiences. They spend money to have fun. They spend money period! Vacations as you know are amazing. Let's make their vacation amazing and make them feel it. Make their stay outstanding.

They could have stayed anywhere but they chose to stay at your property. Why? Ask them. Ask them how their stay is going? Are they excited to be here? Have they had a busy year? Are they ready to relax and enjoy themselves? Lots more "yes" questions. All this will start to come naturally and flow. It may take a few tries to not sound awkward but just remember they are guests in your home so make them feel the love. It's the same if you had friends visiting and wanted to share with them all your favorite places to eat and all the fun activities to do.

The more you like them, the more they will like you. Throw in some compliments when you first meet them. Find anything about them to compliment them on. Seriously. People love to hear about themselves.

Think back the last time you received some random compliment. How did it make you feel? Great right?! Yes!

Now typically we hear compliments from people we know. To hear it from a stranger makes us feel even better. The compliment has to sound sincere or it'll just sound weird. Ask them if it's okay to use their first names and use their first names often. Shake their hands and make them feel welcome.

If they have children ask what their names are. Ask what the kids want to do on vacation. Ask if their excited to be here. Be silly and have fun with the kids. Ask if they'd like to come back. If the kids are into you then the parents are into you.

Find out everything that the guest wants to do. Recall everything from the questions you asked. Now's the time to dig a bit deeper and get some emotion out of them. First, they need to sincerely like you.

Chapter 4 – Make them like you

So you've made friends with your guests and they like you. Now what?

Keep up your energy and it will transfer to your guests. Use your hands a lot. Wave your arms around. Smile often to the point when you get off work you don't want to smile anymore. Silly little things that show excitement. Lots of eye contact. If you already haven't asked who they are traveling with other then their kids ask now. Ask them where they are from and ask them about it. Whatever they say it is the most amazing thing you have ever heard. Be silly but be professional.

You are so excited they are in front of you on vacation. Here's the confusing part. You have to stop and be serious when it comes to discussing why you are recommending something. Be serious when you are discussing directions and activities and dining options. In between all that is your energy.

Take them on a roller coaster of emotions. Up and down, up and down. It's okay to joke around with them but they need to see someone in front of them who knows what they are talking about.

Your confidence needs to be shown. "This is why because….? Do this since….? Doesn't it make more sense to do this because….?"

All of this up and down and confidence and honesty comes across like you have been friends with them for years. This means they are more likely to take your recommendations and suggestions because you are building trust.

Chapter 5 – Build trust

Aside from being a concierge, we need to find out what they want and what they like to do. This comes from being direct with them. Ask what they imagined doing during their vacation? If they have some activity ideas on their own, ask why those activities? It's the same for any other reservation we make. We must find out what their mental picture of their desired activity is. Just ask, it's simple. We do the same for dinner. What do you like to eat? Pair up the restaurant to their needs. So, just pair up the activity with a destination.

Now not only do we need to suggest great recommendations for them, but also some that wouldn't work out for them. Whether it's poor experiences from other guests or perhaps the activity is or isn't child friendly. The reason for this is to establish that we have their best interests in mind. That and well it makes them happy. They're happy and we're happy.

You have to realize that this isn't a smoke and mirrors type of thing. We have nothing to hide. Most guests know they are staying at a timeshare/vacation club resort. At some point they may know someone will ask to have them tour.

The thing is when you come across as someone they like and trust, when you ask them to go on this recommended presentation, they'll be more open-minded about it.

Break the preconceived notion about timeshare. Shatter that stereotype. Bring forth amazing service and establish the friendship and the bond of trust will be easy. Blow them away with how friendly you are. They might even have such a great overall experience that you'll see them every year after and become great acquaintances. Trust me it happens more often than you would realize. Guests will track you down and say hi just for a moment but they will.

This is why we do what we do. This is why we need to open their minds and/or change any opinion about an ownership resort and create great memories for them and a brief friendship. Catch them off guard with your charm and book them on a tour because they might become your new owners. Then who knows? Perhaps you'll see them again.

Chapter 6 – Know your product

If you don't know your program how can you get your guests excited? You will be speaking with owners who have many stories to tell. If not ask them where they have been and how their stay is going. Get them to tell how much they love it.

You can then share those experiences with non-owners. Now the process isn't to tell everything you know. Save that for resistant guests and those who are skeptical. After all the concept of owning your vacations is catching on. We are so used to paying hotel rates or paying a condo owner or using a vacation package from a box store that we forget we are just giving our money away. Why not move your money to your advantage and build some vacation equity. This is vacation ownership at its best.

When getting guests excited you have to be excited. Energy transfers quickly so make sure it's positive energy. It's about the guests 100% of the time. This is why it's vital to understand what you are offering. The details come of course during their presentation.

If your company allows ride alongs with sales agents take them up on it. You will see firsthand how the presentation works and can use that to position the tours you book. Again though don't give away so much that you end up giving a presentation. That is not your job. You get them excited about the ownership, tell them what exactly will happen during the presentation and have them choose a great gift for their time. If you have done your positioning correctly then it improves the odds that they may like what they see during their presentation. Not by much, but sometimes it's just enough. Especially if what you told them on how the presentation will proceed matches up with how it actually goes. Then subconsciously the trust you established with the guest just might trickle over to whoever is presenting the tour and you've got yourself a new owner.

It's all about teasing the guest with untold glories of ownership and any affiliated rewards program. Little nuggets to spark some interest.

"Wouldn't it be nice to fly for free using the same points that you use for free hotel stays?"

"Some of our owners even use their ownership to stay at other villas that are part of an entirely different program."

"Imagine having a vacation home at all the amazing destinations around the world."

"How would it feel to be able send your kids somewhere like the Bahamas for their college graduation present or their honeymoon?"

Start putting creative words together into questions or statements and make a list. Make them fun.

Make some up that would require the guest to put themselves in the picture and or their family. Make some of them extremely emotional.

"After working hard all year long, wouldn't it be nice to know that you have a vacation waiting for you…. so you can leave behind all the stuff that life throws at you so you can reconnect with each other?... Wouldn't that be nice?"

Again. This is all because you know your product. You've spoken with guests and owners and gained insight into their experiences. Felt their emotion. Smiled when you heard a story that melted your heart. Savor these stories from guests and use them as ammo. Your product is more than just an ownership program; it's a way of life for many people. It's a way to rekindle romance. It's a way to unwind and disconnect from the guests' lives and work and all that stuff they deal with. It's a way to create moments with loved ones. It's a way to spend time with their children.

Time moves too fast sometimes so why not paint the picture for your guest on how to slow it down and make memories every single year a week or two at a time. This is your product. If you don't know how your program works then you can't attach an emotional connection to it.

Chapter 7 – As humans we follow trends

People tend to follow what other people are doing. Popular restaurants, clothing, slang, cars, food, everything.

"I have lots of guest who love participating in our presentations. I have guests that come back every year and do a presentation not only for the free gift but to see what's new and especially to see how much better the ownership gets every year. I'm not asking you to go in join our program but if you like vacations and getting more for your vacation dollars then why not go in and see why we have so many people tour with us. Especially to have a personal tour of our property and villas and I'd be happy to set you up with one of these gifts for your experience."

That's just one example and feel to personalize it. Also remember to show that you are paying attention and utilize one or two of whatever gifts you are offering and recommend they take advantage of that gift since it was of interest to them.

Follow it up by asking if they have ever been on a timeshare presentation. Whatever they say…follow up that question with if they have been on a presentation with your company. You only really need to do that if they seem resistant.

This is all important as you can set the expectation of professionalism and passion the whole team has.

Chapter 8 – Asking is easy

Okay so it's not easy if you are just starting out. As you progress it will become second nature. If you don't ask them to tour, two things will happen: it's an automatic "no" when perhaps they were open to touring and the second is that someone else will ask. Either way you lose out on that opportunity and the potential bonus to your paycheck.

As I covered in previous chapters that once you've built that relationship the asking them to tour part will just happen. Sometimes it's towards the end of your interaction and other times it's in the middle.

As you are doing your discovery questions to gather as much information as you can about them you may find your pitch would suit the situation immediately versus later. "Because we're talking about this, there happens to be something else I'd like to offer you. As you probably know we are an ownership property and many of my guests I meet with choose to take part in one of our presentations. Our presentations are fun, interactive and you get to learn about new places and ways to vacation. You'll love hearing about the ways to use the program and we also give you something in return for your time."

You can always followup with "You already said you like to vacation. So why not go in and learn how to take more vacations?"

"I am so glad you chose to stay with us and I know you will have a wonderful vacation. Because you are one of our elite guests we are able to extend an invitation to you to attend one of our property presentations. These are an amazing look into travel with our company. You'll explore new places to stay and an in depth look into how the ownership works. This is a fast paced and very casual tour. It's surprising how many of my guests get involved. I mean it is truly the worlds best travel program...if you like to travel?!... Even my guests who don't get involved always thank me for sending them in. The other great part of your tour is the gift we give your for your time. You can choose from one of these great gifts....Look these over and let me check available times on one of your resort days."

Whatever you say, say it the same every time. Create a script for yourself if one is not provided. Soon whatever you say will sound like yourself. Of course you need to sometimes customize the verbiage depending on your guest in front of you; however, keep it all very similar. Better to have the tidbits at your fingertips and use is it when you need it than not having them at all.

Again, do a ride along with one of the sales staff. You will have the knowledge of what it is like to be on a presentation and you can tell your guests exactly the order of things. If guests have had a poor experience with another company remind them this isn't the case. Tell them you have had guests feel the same way and you always have them find you and share their experience.

Example: "So there will be no surprises while on your presentation, I'll share with you exactly how your experience will go. First, you'll be greeted by our staff and they'll ask some questions to get to know what's important to you so they can personalize the presentation. Next, they will do a quick overview of the property and what's available to you as an owner. Then they will share with you how the program works and then talk about some incentives and pricing. If you fall in love with the program then welcome aboard, if not, then we hope you had a wonderful experience. That's it! There will be no pressure and they even do a survey afterward to make sure you were happy with the experience."

"All our guests leave here happy with a better understanding of vacations like these plus you get one of these fun gifts."

Or more to the point:
Example: "So Bob and Mary it sounds like you enjoy taking vacations. Many of my guests are excited and curious to learn how our ownership works. Did you know this is an ownership property? (It doesn't matter what their answer is.) Are you enjoying the resort? Wonderful! Our presentations are fun and fast paced and always one on one. They'll guide you through our beautiful gallery then you get a personal tour of the property, after that they will share with you how the program works. As always, no pressure. It's easy to mistake passion for pressure especially since we all love what we do. It's a quick 90 minutes and you get to choose an amazing gift for your time."

Alternate choice assumptive close:
"I'd love to have you check it out and if anything just learn about some other places you can stay down the road and have some fun at the same time. We fill up pretty quick since we offer some amazing gifts. I have one spot left for tomorrow morning at 930. That way you can come in and have some coffee and pastries and you'd have the rest of the day to enjoy yourselves or I have a time left for tomorrow afternoon that

way you can enjoy your morning and some sightseeing then come in later. Would you like tomorrow morning or afternoon?"

Yes, sometimes your interactions are a mere 5 minutes or less. That is the fun part. That is your challenge. What to say? When to say it? How to say it?

Chapter 9 – Objections

You'll hear this over and over. Whatever their objections are, that's the reason they should tour. Timeshare, fractional ownership and vacation ownership all generate a fear in guests who aren't familiar with them. The program works. There are many different types of ownership.

It's this lack of knowledge that produces this fear. Oh my gosh it's timeshare. Run for the hills. It's your duty as their concierge, their trusted friend, to be transparent and show them the world of vacations knocking at their door.

Every day we have guests become owners and they love it.

They love it so much that most future business happens to come from existing owners. It's true. Tell the guests to at least give it a look and whether they move forward or not, they have more information to make a decision that will work for them. Many different programs work for many different people.

Objection Examples:
1) No time to tour: Isn't it worth it to take the time to know what your options are when it comes to vacationing more while

spending the same and even less? Vacations after all our time get away from the daily grind of life and reconnect with our loved ones and friendships. 90 minutes is all we ask and your time will open up new doors to travel, places to stay, and introduce you to our program. Remember for us it's about leaving a lasting impression so you'll come visit us time and time again.

2) Not in the market: That's okay. You might surprised be what you can take away from our presentations. Ours are very unique in that they offer more than just the ownership. We have many programs that our loyalty members enjoy for the way they travel. You obviously like to vacation the way you always have. What if for a moment there was a program that could enhance how you currently travel? I bet that would be very interesting to see.

3) Poor past experience: Trust me it's not the first time we've heard these type of experiences. Fortunately for you our company is widely known and is the largest vacation company in the world. I've been with this company for a very long time and rest assured your experience will be amazing.

4) Too busy: That's okay! I'll tell you what though. To spend 90 minutes to learn about the program and learn what's available to you is well worth a lifetime of vacations right? We aren't asking to take up your entire morning or afternoon but only 90 minutes, not 3 or 4 hours. Come in, grab some coffee from our refreshment area and we'll just share with you how it all works. 7 out of 10 reservations here are all owners. They took the time and fell in love. Maybe it's for you, maybe it's not. At least find out what sort of opportunity would be available for you.

5) I need to speak with my spouse: Absolutely you should speak with them...only if you like to vacation with them right? Well let's give them a call. We'll put you down for a tour time and remind your spouse that they are in for a wonderful experience.

Chapter 10 – 3 easy rules to follow

Show up to work on time, book tours and have fun!

www.ingramcontent.com/pod-product-compliance
Lightning Source LLC
Chambersburg PA
CBHW030553220526
45463CB00007B/3073